AmericanGirl Library®

The Mix-It-Up Cookbook

Illustrated by Tracy McGuinness

American Girl®

Published by Pleasant Company Publications

Copyright © 2003 by Pleasant Company

All rights reserved. No part of this book may be used or reproduced in any manner whatsoever
without written permission except in the case of brief quotations embodied in critical articles and reviews.

Questions or comments? Call 1-800-845-0005, or write American Girl, P.O. Box 620497, Middleton, WI 53562-0497.

Visit our Web site at americangirl.com

Printed in Hong Kong.

03 04 05 06 07 08 09 C&C 10 9 8 7 6 5 4 3 2 1

American Girl ® and American Girl Library ® are registered trademarks of Pleasant Company.

Editorial Development: Trula Magruder, Michelle Watkins; Recipe Development: Beth Caldwell Buzogany, Trula Magruder

Art Direction: Camela Decaire, Chris Lorette David; Design: Camela Decaire

Production: Kendra Pulvermacher, Mindy Rappe, Jeannette Bailey; Illustrations: Tracy McGuinness

Photography: Radlund Photography; Food Styling: Beth Caldwell Buzogany

Special thanks to Steve Ingham, Food Safety Extension Specialist

Dear American girl,

Want to know a secret? The more you cook, the better you get. Become comfortable with the basics, then get really creative!

Here's everything you need to "mix it up" in the kitchen.

Know the kitchen rules. Review pages 6 through 10 with a parent.

Learn to make a basic recipe. Start off with a simple, no-fail recipe. Cooking and safety tips help you every step of the way.

Master some mix-ins. Stir simple ingredients into a basic recipe for a brand-new taste!

Keep track! Rate our recipes, record your favorites, or invent new recipes in write-in boxes featured throughout this book.

Make a meal. Treat friends and family to a meal. Once you've decided on a main dish, look for easy side dishes, desserts, and drink recipes, too. Plus, we've added lots of ideas for special days, like Mother's Day or a birthday!

Enjoy!

Your friends at American Girl

table of contents

58 Chocolate

chocolate fondue orange dream • peanut butter kiss • mint cream • fruit whip • chocolate caramel • mock mounds **chocolate chip cookies** double chocolate • berry white • double nut • peanut butter cup • butterscotch bites • m&m chews **chocolate pudding** dessert dip • oreo mousse • bear pair pudding **dessert dominoes**

68 popcorn

old-fashioned popcorn cheese pleaser • kettle korn • tex mix • movie madness • pucker popper • peanut butter cup **popcorn balls** fuddy nutty • confetti balls • crunch bars **garden pops**

76 ice cream

girlie-swirlie shakes chocolate monkey • maple milk shake • soy power plus • cookies 'n' cream • white whopper • pink flamingo **ice cream sandwiches** mint cooler • oatburst • mini rainbow • polar pop-tarts • gooey grahams • brrrr-berry **very cool cupcakes**

84 mix a meal

drinks eye-opener smoothie • sparkling lemonade • fruit frappé • pineapple punch • mango lhassi • cranberry splash **soups and salads** italian flag salad • cream of broccoli • bits-and-bites salad • quick tomato topper • bunny slaw • hot potato! soup **simple sides** fruit kabobs • hash browns • pink clouds • celery stuffers • six-star salad • fried corn **sweets** mud puddles • candied marshmallows • sunrise salute • peanutty crisp • jell-o jewels • iced cranberry creams **set a basic table** show-off tabletops

kitchen tools

1. Ask an adult to go through this list with you, checking off the kitchen appliances and tools you can use.

2. Before cooking, review your recipe and your checklist to see if an adult needs to help you.

3. If you need an adult to help make a particular recipe, set a time that will work for both of you.

4. Pull back long hair. Then, to keep drips and spills off your clothes, tie on an apron, and get cooking!

O.K. to use . . .	with an adult	by yourself	never—always ask an adult
Stovetop	☐	☐	☐
Oven	☐	☐	☐
Microwave	☐	☐	☐
Blender	☐	☐	☐
Electric Mixer	☐	☐	☐
Sharp Knives	☐	☐	☐
Cheese Grater	☐	☐	☐

Even if you're allowed to use the stovetop, never handle a pot of boiling water. Always ask an adult for help!

kitchen skills

1. Ask an adult to go through this list with you.

2. If you don't know a skill, ask an adult to set aside time and show you what you want to learn.

3. If a parent plans to prepare a part of the recipe for you, check to see if she or he will be ready to help when you start cooking.

Chef Skills	I know this.	Adult will show me.	Don't know. An adult will do this for me.
Which dishware can be used in a microwave			
How to use a colander			
How to slice and dice fruit			
How to slice and dice vegetables			
How to use potholders with heavy cookware			
How to cook meat for a recipe			
How to flip pancakes and other foods			

kitchen care

Let food cool down in a microwave before removing. Containers can be very hot!

Read your recipe carefully to make sure you have everything. Set out tools and measure and chop ingredients. Imagine you're on a cooking show and everything must be ready when cameras roll!

Pull back hair, remove jewelry, and slip on an apron.

To slice vegetables, use a cutting board to protect the counter.

Keep pot handles turned in.

Keep a dry potholder handy.

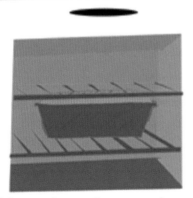

Put large pans on large burners and small pans on small burners.

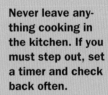

Never leave anything cooking in the kitchen. If you must step out, set a timer and check back often.

Before you turn on the oven, make sure nothing is inside, then adjust the racks. Turn off oven as soon as you're done.

Wipe up spills immediately. Not only is it safer, but cleanup will be easier later.

Before starting, wash hands with soap and warm water, and wipe off counters with a soapy sponge. Also wash hands before and after handling meat.

Never touch electrical plugs or a socket with wet hands.

It's safer to cook with an adult. A parent should always know you are in the kitchen!

Wash all fruits and vegetables well.

Always ask an adult to handle hot, heavy pans or boiling liquids. Never do this yourself!

Don't slip a sharp object into soapy water. Someone might get cut because she can't see it.

To make cleanup even easier, ask an adult to show you how to use a dishwasher properly!

Try to keep pets away from cooking areas.

chef smarts

cutting fruits or vegetables: never use the same board you use for raw meat or poultry.

1. Lay fruit or vegetable on a cutting board, and hold it with the hand you don't write with. Keep fingers tucked under.

2. Hold the knife in your writing hand by "shaking hands" with the handle. Don't use a dull knife or the blade could slip.

3. Place the knife blade across the top of the vegetable. Slowly draw the blade down and back toward you to make a slice.

4. Lay the slice flat, turn it, and cut across it to make a strip. Slice the strips to dice.

measuring dry ingredients: use a scooping cup.

1. Scoop up ingredient to lightly fill the measuring cup or spoon. If you're measuring brown sugar, pack it in tightly.

2. With the edge of a butter knife, scrape evenly across the top of the cup or spoon to remove the excess ingredient.

amounts: when measuring less than ¼ cup, use measuring spoons.

a pinch = less than ¼ teaspoon

a dash = a few drops

3 teaspoons = 1 tablespoon

2 tablespoons = 1 liquid ounce

4 tablespoons = 2 liquid ounces = ¼ cup

8 tablespoons = 4 liquid ounces = ½ cup

1 cup = ½ pint = 8 liquid ounces = 16 tablespoons

2 cups = 1 pint (liquid) or 1 pound (dry) = 16 ounces

4 cups = 2 pints = 1 quart = 32 liquid ounces

4 quarts = 1 gallon

measuring liquid ingredients: use a clear cup.

1. Place the measuring cup on a counter. Pour liquid into the cup.

2. Bend down so your eye is even with mark at amount you're measuring. Liquid should be level with mark. If it isn't, add more or pour some out and check again.

chef tips

- Use a flour sifter to spread flour over a surface for kneading pizza dough.

- If you're concerned you might scratch a pan's surface, use a wooden spoon to stir.

- To soften brown sugar, cover in a bowl, then microwave on high for 30 seconds.

- Keep onions in the refrigerator's vegetable crisper or slip them into the freezer for 30 minutes, and you won't "cry" when you're cutting them.

- Spray spatulas, spoons, or other tools with cooking spray to keep batter, dough, or other foods from sticking to them.

- Sprinkle milk over dried-out coconut flakes. Let sit a few minutes to remoisten coconut. Use immediately!

- To "chop" whole nuts, slip them into a zippered plastic bag, then roll over them with a rolling pin.

- Make extra pasta, then store 1-cup servings in the freezer to serve with the single-serving sauces on page 51!

- To keep marshmallows from sticking to your hands when making popcorn balls, rub hands with butter, run them under cold water, or spray them with cooking spray.

- If you drop an egg on the floor, pour salt over it. This "gels" the egg, so it's easier to wipe up with a paper towel.

chef terms

baking powder An ingredient used to help dough or batter rise. Don't confuse this with baking soda!

beat To stir quickly with a spoon, whisk, or electric mixer to thoroughly mix ingredients.

brown sugar Sugar that has not had the molasses removed. It comes in both light and dark varieties. When a recipe in this book calls for brown sugar, use light.

cocoa Unsweetened powdered chocolate. Hot chocolate or hot cocoa mix is chocolate powder that's sweetened with sugar and milk. If a recipe calls for cocoa, use unsweetened cocoa!

cooked meat If a recipe calls for cooked meat, use leftovers or precooked meat sold in the grocery, or ask an adult to help you cook the meat before starting the recipe.

cream To combine foods (such as butter and sugar) until they are fluffy.

fold To gently add a light ingredient (like nuts) into a heavier mixture (like pancake batter) without beating or stirring. Use a spoon or rubber spatula to turn the heavier mixture over on top of the lighter ingredient, working your way around the bowl.

heavy whipping cream A liquid cream, found in the dairy case, that is rich enough to be whipped.

powdered sugar Also called confectioner's sugar. A very fine sugar used mostly for desserts.

preheat To turn on the oven so that it warms to the desired temperature. It's important to preheat the oven before putting food in to bake.

sauté To brown or cook food quickly in a pan with a fat such as oil or butter.

vanilla A liquid flavoring. Most recipes call for pure vanilla extract, but imitation vanilla flavoring can be used as well.

whipped cream An aerosol-spray whipped cream. In our recipes, a nondairy topping, such as Cool Whip, will work fine.

eggs

AGED CHEDDAR

eggs

12

eggs

scrambled eggs

To scramble eggs for a flock of friends, use two eggs per person.

stovetop

1. Crack 2 eggs into a small bowl. Add a dash of salt and pepper. Beat with a fork until yellow and frothy. Put ½ tablespoon butter into a nonstick pan. Heat on medium-high until butter bubbles. Pour in eggs.

2. Push eggs from outside edges to center of pan with a wooden spoon, scraping eggs off sides of pan as you stir. Once eggs thicken, remove pan from heat.

here's how!
To crack an egg, tap it against a bowl rim. Gently push your thumbs into the crack, and pull apart the halves over the bowl. Toss the shells. Wash hands with soap and warm water.

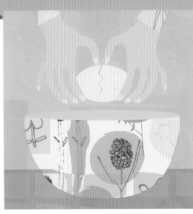

microwave

Place 2 eggs and a dash of salt and pepper into a microwavable bowl. Beat with a fork until yellow and frothy. Microwave on high for 1 minute. Stir, then repeat. Let cool. Fluff with a fork. (Some microwaves may need a longer cooking time.)

For a cheerful breakfast, serve Confetti Eggs on a pretty platter!

mix-ins

Pour 2 eggs into a pan, then add these ingredients before you scramble them!

cheesy trio
**1 tablespoon grated Swiss;
1 tablespoon grated cheddar;
1 tablespoon grated
Monterey Jack cheese**

showy salmon
**¼ cup smoked salmon;
3 tablespoons cream cheese;
2 tablespoons diced green onions**

sunny aloha
**1 pineapple ring, chopped;
1 tablespoon red bell pepper**

confetti eggs
**1 tablespoon each of diced red,
yellow, and green bell peppers**

pepperoni pizza
**¼ cup grated mozzarella cheese;
2 tablespoons pizza sauce;
6 slices pepperoni, chopped**

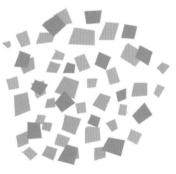

ham 'n' eggs
3 tablespoons diced ham

chef's journal

Kitchen Notes

Mmm! I liked these eggs best:

Next time I want to try adding

Here's my recipe:

15

boiled eggs

Have a crack at hard-cooked eggs!

stovetop

1. With an adult's help, put eggs into a pan with enough cold water to cover them. Place pan uncovered on burner, and turn to high. Bring to a boil.

2. Turn off heat and cover eggs with a lid. Let sit for 15 minutes for large eggs and 20 minutes for extra-large eggs. When time is up, ask an adult to pour off hot water and run cold water over eggs until they cool down.

mix-ins

With three basic condiments, you can make deviled eggs, egg salad, or egg salad sandwiches!

deviled eggs

Peel 6 boiled eggs. Slice in half lengthwise with a knife. Bend each egg white slightly so that yolk pops into a medium bowl. Place whites on a plate. Mash yolks with a fork until crumbly. Mix in 1 tablespoon yellow mustard and 2 tablespoons each of mayonnaise and sweet pickle relish. Fill egg white with yolk mixture. Sprinkle on paprika! Serves 3.

egg salad

Peel and chop 6 boiled eggs. Scoop eggs into a medium bowl. Mix in 1 tablespoon yellow mustard, 2 tablespoons each of mayonnaise and sweet pickle relish. (For a fancier salad, also add 2 tablespoons each of diced celery and onions.) Place each serving on a lettuce leaf or in a hollowed-out tomato. Serves 4.

egg sandwich

Cut crusts off 2 slices of bread with a butter knife. Spread egg salad between slices. Cut sandwich diagonally twice, making 4 finger sandwiches. Tip: Serve on toast for a breakfast treat! Serves 1.

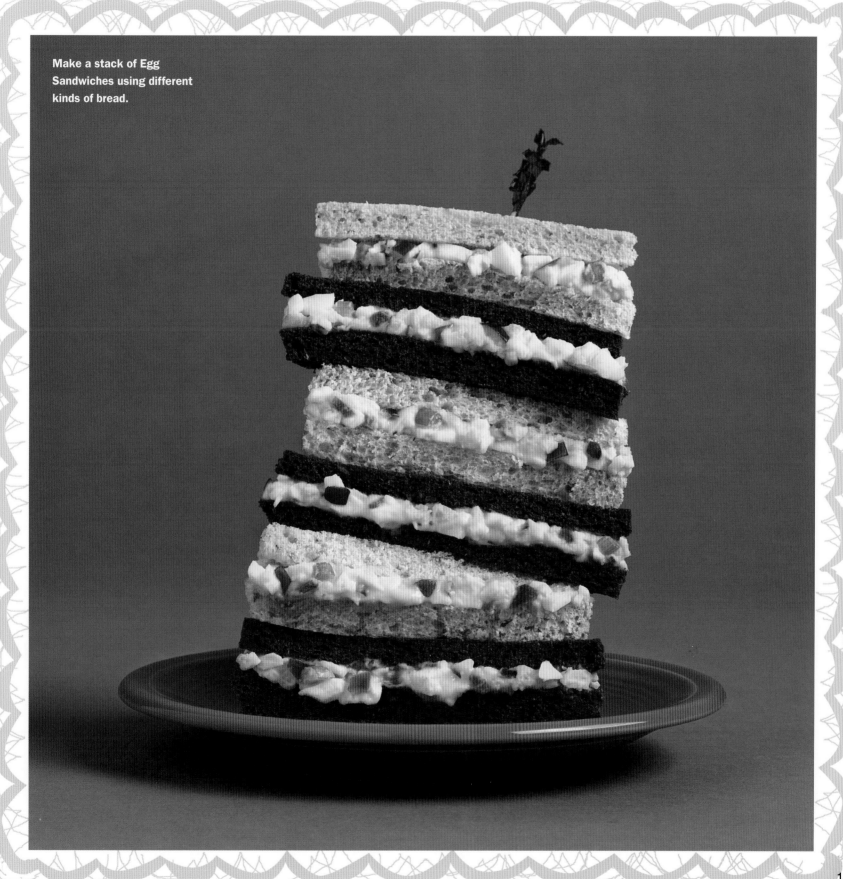

Make a stack of Egg
Sandwiches using different
kinds of bread.

Serve these itty egg nests on tiny plates. Sprinkle on minced parsley for added color and flavor.

chef's special!

egg nests

you will need

- an adult
- muffin tin
- cooking spray
- 6 large slices white bread, crusts removed
- rolling pin
- 6 tablespoons diced ham
- 6 tablespoons shredded cheddar cheese
- 6 eggs
- small bowl
- fork
- salt and pepper
- baking dish (be sure muffin tin fits inside)
- plates

1. Preheat oven to 400 degrees. Coat 6 sections of a muffin tin with cooking spray. Press each bread slice down hard with a rolling pin to flatten. Tuck a slice into each muffin cup. Be sure all 4 corners of bread slice stick out over rim.

2. Sprinkle 1 tablespoon ham into each nest. Top with 1 tablespoon cheddar cheese. Crack an egg into a bowl, stir with a fork, then pour into a nest. Repeat with each nest. Sprinkle on salt and pepper.

3. With an adult's help, fill a baking dish half full with water, and place muffin tin in it. Carefully slip dish onto middle rack in oven. Bake 25 minutes or longer until eggs cook through.

4. Ask an adult to remove pan from oven, being careful not to spill water into muffin tin. Let cool slightly.

5. Remove nests and slip them onto plates. Serves 6.

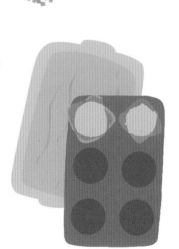

pancakes

Pancakes, hotcakes, flapjacks, or griddle cakes—whatever you call them, they're a favorite everywhere!

stovetop

1. In a medium bowl, mix **1 cup** all-purpose flour, **¼ teaspoon** salt, **1 tablespoon** sugar, **and 2 teaspoons** baking powder.

2. In a small bowl, combine **1 beaten** egg, **1 cup** milk, **and 2 tablespoons** cooking oil. **Stir into dry ingredients. Beat with a** whisk **just until batter is moist but still lumpy.**

3. Turn burner to medium heat. Pour 1 teaspoon cooking oil **into** pan. **Test pan temperature. If it's ready, add ½ cup batter.**

here's how!
To test the temperature, sprinkle a little water on the pan. If the water skitters around and then evaporates, it's perfect!

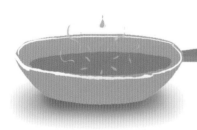

4. Watch for batter bubbles! After lots pop, flip pancake with a spatula, **but don't press it down! This will make pancake tough, not fluffy.**

5. After 1 minute, lift edge of pancake. If it's golden brown on bottom, remove it and make another one. Makes 4 to 6 pancakes.

To make lots of pancakes, triple your recipe. So instead of 1 cup of flour, add 3 cups. Multiply all your other ingredients by 3, too!

mix-ins

Open up a pancake café! Just add these ingredients to your batter.

apple pie

1 cup chunky natural applesauce;
1 teaspoon nutmeg. Serve with
butter, cinnamon, and sugar.

pbj

½ cup peanut butter mixed with
4 tablespoons very hot water.
Serve with jelly.

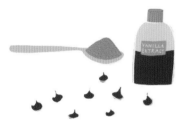

chippers

1 cup chocolate chips;
½ teaspoon vanilla;
1 tablespoon sugar. Serve with a
dollop of whipped cream.

crunchy cakes

1 cup chopped pecans;
2 tablespoons brown sugar.
Serve with maple syrup.

mock muffins

2 bananas, mashed;
¼ cup poppy seeds.
Serve with applesauce.

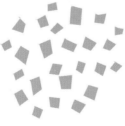

pig in a blanket

1 cup diced ham.
Serve with
maple syrup.

Pancake Report Card

Make these pancakes, then give
them a grade!

A = Awesome!

B = Better than I expected.

C = Could do in a pinch.

D = Don't even go there!

F = Fooooey!

Subject	Grade	Comments
apple pie	☐	
pbj	☐	
chippers	☐	
crunchy cakes	☐	
mock muffins	☐	
pig in a blanket	☐	

23

chef's special!

you will need
- pancake batter, from page 22
- clean, squeezable bottle
- pan or griddle
- spatula
- plate
- whipped cream
- favorite flavor of jelly or jam

petal pancakes

1. Make pancake batter. Fill squeezable bottle with batter.

2. Heat pan on medium-high until water drops sizzle and evaporate. Using the bottle, outline 5 egg-sized petals on pan, then squeeze in batter to fill. (You may have room for only 2 or 3 at a time.) Once petals brown, flip them over and brown the other side.

3. Arrange petals on a plate. Drop a dollop of whipped cream in the center, then top with jelly or jam.

For a flower garden,
try different flavors of jam!

25

quick
breads

FRESH MILK

RAISINS

quick breads

ALL PURPOSE FLOUR

VEG OIL

tea bread

For that perfect teatime snack, serve thin slices of banana bread.

oven

1. Preheat oven to 350 degrees. In a large bowl, add 1 cup all-purpose flour, ½ cup bran flakes cereal, ¾ cup sugar, 1 teaspoon baking powder, ½ teaspoon cinnamon, and ¼ teaspoon nutmeg. Stir until well blended.

2. In a medium bowl, beat 2 eggs with a fork until foamy. Add ¼ cup cooking oil. Mash 2 ripe bananas. Add bananas to eggs and oil, and mix well.

3. Pour banana mixture over dry ingredients, and stir with a spoon until flour is just moistened. Batter should be lumpy and thick.

4. Spray an 8-by-4-inch loaf pan with cooking spray. Pour batter into pan. Bake 40 to 50 minutes until done. With an adult's help, remove bread from oven and let cool in pan for 10 minutes; then turn it out onto a rack. Let cool before slicing.

here's how!

Not sure if your bread is done? Use oven mitts to pull the rack out of the oven slightly. Stick a butter knife into the center of the pan. If it comes out without batter on it, the bread's done!

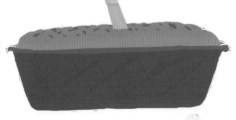

For a showy loaf, fill a pastry or plastic bag with icing, then squiggle on a decorative top!

mix-ins

Fold these ingredients into your batter for the greatest thing since sliced bread!

nut bread
**1 cup sweetened coconut flakes;
1 cup chopped pecans**

chewy chocolate chip
1 cup semisweet chocolate chips

juicy fruit
**1 cup canned crushed pineapple,
drained; 1 cup canned mango,
drained**

island loaf
**¾ cup chopped macadamia nuts;
1 cup sweetened coconut flakes**

orchard cake
**replace bananas with 1 cup
chunky applesauce; ½ cup raisins;
½ cup chopped walnuts**

overly orange
**replace bananas with ¾ cup
orange juice; 1 cup Orange Slices
candy, chopped;
½ cup chopped pecans**

french toast

Powdered sugar, maple syrup, or berries and cream will make French toast taste like a dream!

stovetop

In a pie pan, **beat 2** eggs, **¼ cup** milk, **1 teaspoon** sugar, **½ teaspoon** vanilla, **and ¼ teaspoon** cinnamon **until well blended. Pour 1 teaspoon** oil **into a** skillet **and heat on medium. Dip 2 slices of** bread **into egg mixture and place in skillet. Cook until golden brown, then flip with a** spatula **and cook other side. Serves 1.**

here's how!

Drop a slice of bread into egg mixture. With a fork, press on bread until it's coated. Then carefully pick up slice with a fork or your fingers, flip it over, and coat other side. Repeat with second slice.

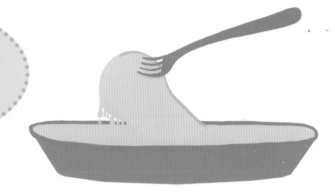

mix-ins

For a special toast, try these big dippers!

pbj dipper

Make a peanut butter sandwich. **Dip sandwich in** basic french toast egg mixture, **and cook as shown above. Top with** jelly. **Serves 1.**

monte cristo

Make a cold ham and cheese sandwich. **Dip sandwich in** basic french toast egg mixture, **and cook as shown above. Serves 1.**

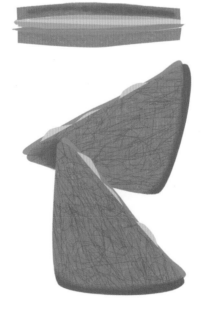

français toast

In a small bowl, **mix 2 tablespoons softened** cream cheese **and 1 tablespoon** orange marmalade. **Set aside. Using 2 slices** French bread, **make a serving of** basic french toast, **and cook as shown above. Spread cheese mixture on top of each slice, then sprinkle on** powdered sugar. **Serves 1.**

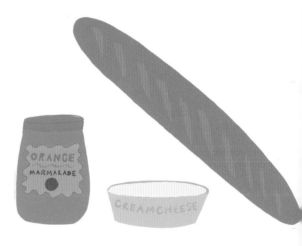

For a perfect dusting of powdered sugar, sprinkle it on with a tea strainer or flour sifter.

Fill a table with these tiny treats,
and then say, "Bonbon appétit!"

bonbon banana cream pie muffins

you will need

- banana bread batter from page 28
- bonbon cups, available in baking aisle of grocery
- mini muffin tins
- spoon
- 8 ounces cream cheese, softened
- ¼ cup honey
- small bowl
- butter knife
- sprinkles
- whipped cream

1. Make banana bread batter, following recipe from page 28.

2. Place bonbon cups into mini muffin tins. Spoon batter into cups (or fill regular muffin tins ½ full with batter).

3. Bake for 7 to 8 minutes, or until golden brown. With an adult's help, remove muffins from oven. Let cool.

4. Combine cream cheese and honey in bowl. Mix well. Spread thickly on top of muffins with knife.

5. Add sprinkles. Top with a dollop of whipped cream. Serve immediately.

pizza

pizza

This pizzeria-style crust takes about 2 hours total to prepare, but you'll have so much fun, you won't mind the wait!

oven

1. Preheat oven to 400 degrees. In a medium bowl, mix ¾ cup warm water with 1 package dry yeast. Add ¼ teaspoon salt, 1 tablespoon olive oil, and 2 cups all-purpose flour. Mix with a wooden spoon; then, as dough gets stiff, use your hands. If dough is sticky, mix in a little flour. If it's dry, sprinkle on water. Drop dough onto a floured surface and knead it for 5 minutes.

here's how!

To knead, hold dough with one hand while you push it away from you with the other. Then fold it back on itself. Work dough until it feels smooth and elastic.

2. Coat a large bowl with cooking spray. Place dough in bowl and cover with plastic wrap. Keep in a warm spot for 1 hour.

3. Spill dough onto a floured surface, punch dough, and then shape it into a big ball. Let rest for 15 minutes.

4. Dust your clean hands with flour, then press the edges of the dough to flatten it until it's about the size of your pizza pan. Spray pan with cooking spray, then lay dough on it. Add toppings.

5. Brush oil on crust edges. Bake for 25 minutes or until crust is crispy. With an adult's help, remove pizza from oven and cut it into slices.

Let guests choose their favorite toppings, such as Hula Ham, Sweet Garden, or Barbecued Chicken.

mix-ins

Pile these toppings onto an unbaked crust to give your pizza pizzazz!

pepperoni pie
¾ cup pizza sauce;
3 cups shredded mozzarella;
3-ounce package
pepperoni slices

hula ham
½ cup pizza sauce mixed with
¼ cup teriyaki barbecue sauce;
3 cups shredded mozzarella;
1 cup pineapple chunks, drained;
1 cup diced ham

sweet garden
¾ cup pizza sauce;
3 cups shredded mozzarella;
½ cup sliced mushrooms;
½ cup bell peppers;
½ cup onions; ½ cup black olives

triple cheese
¾ cup pizza sauce;
1 cup shredded mozzarella;
1 cup shredded provolone;
½ cup grated parmesan

veggie-roni
¾ cup pizza sauce;
2½ cups shredded
mozzarella-style soy cheese;
1 package soy pepperoni slices

barbecued chicken
½ cup pizza sauce mixed with
¼ cup barbecue sauce;
2½ cups shredded mozzarella;
2 cups cooked diced chicken

37

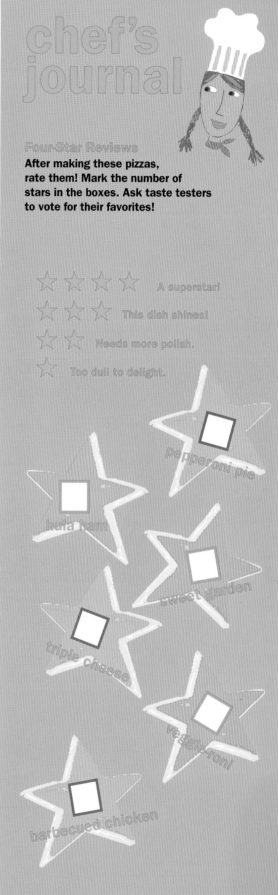

chef's journal

Four-Star Reviews
After making these pizzas,
rate them! Mark the number of
stars in the boxes. Ask taste testers
to vote for their favorites!

☆ ☆ ☆ ☆ A superstar!
☆ ☆ ☆ This dish shines!
☆ ☆ Needs more polish.
☆ Too dull to delight.

pepperoni pie
hula ham
sweet garden
triple cheese
veggie-roni
barbecued chicken

chef's special!

apple pizza pie

you will need

- crust for pizza from page 36
- pizza pan
- cooking spray
- ½ cup granulated sugar
- 6 Golden Delicious apples
- paring knife
- 1 stick butter
- medium pot
- 1 cup brown sugar
- 1 teaspoon cinnamon
- ½ cup dried cranberries
- slotted spoon
- pizza cutter
- whipped cream or ice cream, if desired

1. Prepare crust for pizza, and spread onto a pizza pan. Spray crust with cooking spray, then sprinkle on granulated sugar. Bake crust for 25 minutes or until golden.

2. With an adult's help, peel, core, and thinly slice apples. Melt butter in pot over medium-high heat. Pour in brown sugar, stirring until dissolved. Add apples and cinnamon and bring to a boil.

3. Turn heat down to low and simmer for 5 to 7 minutes or until apples are softened. Stir in cranberries. Remove from heat and let cool.

4. Using slotted spoon, carefully scoop apples onto crust, leaving juice in pan.

5. Slice and serve with whipped cream or ice cream, if desired.

For a special occasion, shape a simple flower on top with cooked apples and cranberries!

tortillas

quesadillas

Grab a taste of the Southwest with this chewy, cheesy turnover!

stovetop

1. Combine ½ cup shredded cheddar and ½ cup shredded Monterey Jack cheeses in a small bowl.

2. Spread wax paper on counter, then lay out 4 small flour tortillas in a single layer. Sprinkle ¼ cup cheese on right side of each tortilla. Fold tortillas in half.

3. Spray a large pan with cooking spray, then preheat pan on medium-high. Add quesadilla, and heat for 1 or 2 minutes to melt cheese and lightly brown. Use a spatula to flip over quesadilla and brown other side. Repeat with remaining quesadillas. Cut into triangles. Serve warm with your favorite sides. Serves 2 to 4.

here's how!
Set out small bowls of toppings that complement a quesadilla, such as sour cream, salsa, black olives, shredded lettuce, or guacamole.

Don't worry if the fillings spill out of the tortilla, as they do in this Country Quesa. That only makes them look tastier!

mix-ins

Add these ingredients to 1 cheesy quesadilla before cooking it.

olé burger

¼ cup cooked hamburger or soy
burger; 2 tablespoons chopped
onion; dash of pepper

sweet-tart

¼ cup golden raisins; ¼ cup dried
cranberries; dash of allspice

brown betty

¼ cup thinly sliced apples;
1 teaspoon brown sugar;
dash of cinnamon

chili pie

replace Monterey Jack cheese
with Pepper Jack cheese;
¼ cup canned chili;
1 tablespoon diced green onions

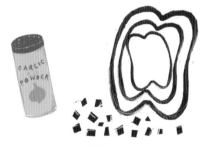

country quesa

¼ cup cooked, chopped chicken;
¼ cup diced red bell peppers;
dash of garlic powder

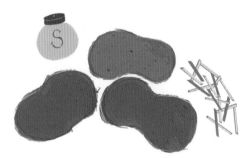

potato pocket

¼ cup cooked hash browns;
2 tablespoons crispy bacon or
bacon bits; dash of salt

---

chef's journal

Kitchen Notes

Mmm! I liked these quesadillas best:

....

....

....

....

Next time I want to try adding

....

....

....

....

Here's my recipe:

....

....

....

....

....

....

....

ready to wrap

To keep your wrap rolled up tight, follow these easy folding instructions.

countertop

1. Center fillings on a warm or cold large flour tortilla. **Lay** fillings **such as cheeses, spreads, or cold cuts flat on bottom. Add sauces last.**

2. Fold 1 end over toward center.

3. Fold the bottom flap up.

4. Starting at the bottom, roll up entire tortilla. Eat like a burrito.

For a fancy wrap, try flavored tortillas with the Chinese Chicken Salad, Egg Salad Sub, or Bird on the Greens!

mix-ins

Have a wrap session! Bring out the tortillas, the fixings, and a whole lot of friends!

morning wrap

1 slice American cheese; 1 slice
deli ham; 1 microwaved egg
(See "Microwave," page 14);
1 teaspoon salsa

bird on the greens

2 teaspoons honey mustard;
2 slices deli turkey or soy turkey;
fresh spinach leaves;
½ avocado, sliced

banana nut

2 tablespoons peanut butter;
1 small banana, sliced;
drizzle of honey

bologna burrito

1 lettuce leaf; 1 slice bologna;
1 slice American cheese;
1 teaspoon salsa

chinese chicken salad

1 Chinese cabbage leaf;
½ cup cooked, diced chicken;
2 tablespoons bean sprouts;
2 teaspoons Asian-style dressing;
top with chow mein noodles

egg salad sub

2 dry lettuce leaves;
½ cup egg salad from page 16

chef's journal

Wrap Report Card
Make these wraps, then give them
a grade!

A = Awesome!

B = Better than I thought.

C = Could do in a pinch.

D = Don't even go there!

F = Fooooey!

Subject	Grade	Comments
morning wrap	☐	
bird on the greens	☐	
banana nut	☐	
bologna burrito	☐	
chinese chicken salad	☐	
egg salad sub	☐	

45

Experiment with different star sizes and colored sugars for a star-spangled sundae!

46

chef's special!

cinna-star sundae

you will need
- flour tortillas
- cutting board
- star-shaped cookie cutter, 2 to 3 inches across
- cookie sheet
- 1 teaspoon cinnamon
- ½ cup granulated or colored sugar
- small bowl
- cooking spray
- spoon
- vanilla ice cream
- ice cream scoop
- parfait dish
- fresh raspberries
- whipped cream

1. Preheat oven to 400 degrees. Lay tortillas on cutting board, and cut out as many stars as needed with cookie cutter. (If it's too difficult to cut stars with cookie cutter, use cookie cutter to make an impression on tortilla, then cut out design with kitchen scissors.) Lay stars on cookie sheet.

2. Mix cinnamon and sugar in bowl. Spray tortillas with cooking spray.

3. Use a spoon to sprinkle some stars with cinnamon and sugar and some with just colored sugar. Bake 3 to 5 minutes until crisp and slightly browned.

4. Scoop vanilla ice cream into a dish. Add raspberries. Top with whipped cream. Stand several stars in ice cream. Use red, white, and blue sugars for a patriotic parfait!

noodles

pasta bar

Pick a pasta, then pair it with a favorite sauce for a quick lunch or dinner!

stovetop

1. Figure out the number of pasta servings needed. Check noodle package for amounts of pasta and water. In a large saucepan, bring water to a boil on high. Add pasta. Lower heat to medium-high. Cook uncovered, stirring occasionally.

2. Put a colander in the sink. With an adult's help, hold pan handles with oven mitts. Pour pasta and water into the colander to drain. Rinse. Drain again. Pour pasta into a bowl. Spoon a pasta sauce on top.

here's how!
Ask an adult to very slowly and carefully tilt pot away from you as you pour, so water doesn't splatter on you. Watch out for the hot steam!

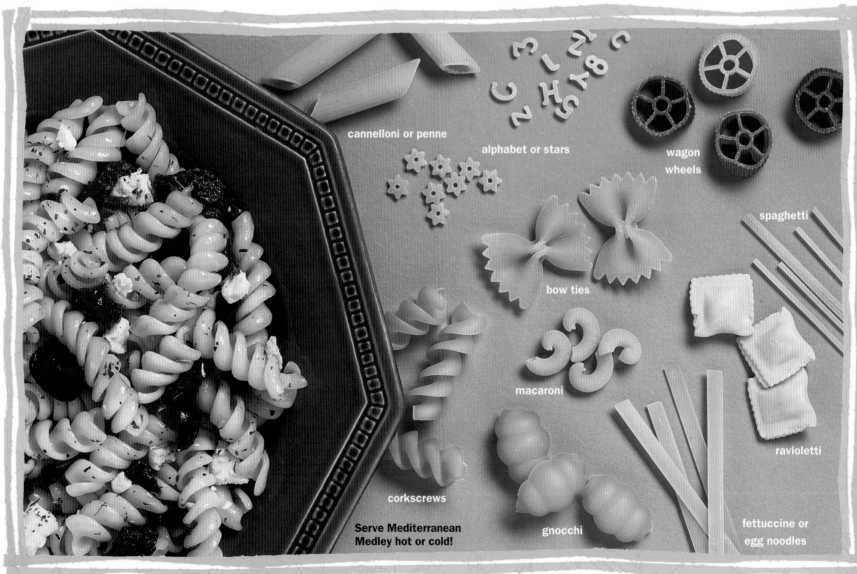

cannelloni or penne

alphabet or stars

wagon wheels

spaghetti

bow ties

macaroni

ravioletti

corkscrews

gnocchi

fettuccine or egg noodles

Serve Mediterranean Medley hot or cold!

mix-ins

Pour one of these sauces over a single serving of cooked pasta for a *"Ciao, Italia!"* meal.

presto pesto
1 tablespoon pesto sauce; ½ cup fresh or canned chopped tomatoes. Heat on medium.

white sauce
¼ cup heavy whipping cream; 1 tablespoon butter; 1 tablespoon grated Parmesan cheese. Heat on medium. Let stand to thicken.

picnic pasta salad
1 tablespoon chopped red bell pepper; 1 tablespoon broccoli; 1 tablespoon celery; 2 tablespoons Italian dressing. Pour over pasta and chill.

asian pasta salad
¼ cup shredded cabbage; ¼ cup carrots; 2 tablespoons thinly sliced onions; 2 tablespoons chopped peanuts; ¼ cup Asian-style salad dressing. Pour over pasta and chill.

brocco-cheez
4 ounces pasteurized processed cheese, like Velveeta or Cheez Whiz; ½ cup cooked chopped broccoli. Heat on medium.

mediterranean medley
¼ cup sun-dried tomatoes in oil, drained and chopped; ¼ cup feta cheese; 1 tablespoon sliced black olives; ½ teaspoon dried oregano; ½ teaspoon garlic salt

chef's journal

Pasta House
Take notes of your friends' and family's favorite pastas. On a birthday or other special day, serve a plate of pasta!

guest check

Name	Favorite Pasta	Comments

51

macaroni and cheese

Create quite a stir making mac and cheese from scratch!

stovetop

1. In a large pot, bring 6 cups water to a full boil over high heat. Add 16 ounces elbow macaroni, then reduce heat to medium-high. Cook 7 to 10 minutes, stirring occasionally until tender. Ask an adult to pour noodles into a colander to drain, then place in serving bowl. Set aside.

2. In a small saucepan, melt 3 tablespoons butter over low heat. Add ¼ cup all-purpose flour and ½ teaspoon salt. Cook for 3 minutes, stirring constantly. Sauce should be as thick as paste.

3. Raise heat to medium-high. Add 2 cups milk. Cook for about 5 minutes, stirring constantly until sauce thickens.

4. Sprinkle in 2 cups shredded cheddar cheese and ½ cup grated Parmesan cheese. Stir until melted. Pour sauce over elbow noodles, then stir until well mixed. Serves 6 to 8.

FRESH MILK

Moo

here's how!

Pour in ½ cup of milk at a time. Stir quickly until the flour mixture is completely smooth. You don't want any lumps or milk to stick to the bottom of the pan.

For a simple meal, serve a bowl of Tasty Tuna with a small salad or sliced fruit.

mix-ins

To create a stovetop casserole, stir these ingredients into cooked mac and cheese.

tasty tuna
two 6-ounce cans tuna, drained;
1 cup frozen petite peas, heated in
microwave for 5 minutes,
then drained

veggie stroganoff
4 veggie burgers, crumbled,
heated in pan; ½ cup sour cream;
¼ teaspoon paprika

mexican casserole
1 cup chunky salsa; 15-ounce can
whole-kernel corn, drained;
2 teaspoons taco seasoning

island macaroni
1½ cups chopped ham;
8-ounce can pineapple tidbits,
well drained

garden medley
16-ounce package frozen
vegetables (such as broccoli,
cauliflower, and carrot medley) and
2 tablespoons water heated in
microwave for 8 to 10 minutes,
then drained

pizza mac
½ pound ground beef cooked and
drained; 8-ounce can pizza sauce;
1 teaspoon Italian seasoning

chef's journal

Four-Star Reviews
After cooking these pastas, rate
them! Mark the number of stars in
the boxes. Ask taste testers to vote
for their favorites!

★ ★ ★ ★   A superstar!

★ ★ ★   This dish shines!

★ ★   Needs more polish.

★   Too dull to delight.

tasty tuna

veggie stroganoff

mexican casserole

island macaroni

garden medley

pizza mac

spaghetti marinara

If you're in the mood for something light, this meatless sauce is *fantastico!*

stovetop

1. Place **2 tablespoons** olive oil in a large pan. **Turn heat to medium-high, then cook ½ cup finely chopped** onion **until nearly clear, about 3 minutes. Add a 29-ounce can** tomato sauce **and 2 table-spoons** tomato paste **to pan. Stir well, then lower heat to medium.**

2. Add **½ teaspoon** garlic powder, **1 teaspoon** Italian seasoning, **1 tablespoon chopped** parsley, **and 1 teaspoon** salt. **Simmer for 5 minutes on low. With an adult's help, cook a package of** spaghetti, **following instructions on page 50.** Spoon **sauce over noodles. Serves 6.**

mix-ins

Give marinara a makeover! Simply add these ingredients to the sauce shown above.

sunset sauce

Pour an 8-ounce carton of heavy whipping cream **into cooled marinara sauce. Stir constantly over medium-low heat until warmed through. With an adult's help, cook a package of** gnocchi pasta, **following instructions on page 50.** Spoon **sauce over noodles.**

mini meatballs

With an adult's help, mix 1 pound lean ground beef, **½ cup finely chopped** onion, **1** egg, **and 1 teaspoon** salt **in a** medium bowl. **Shape marble-sized meatballs with clean hands. Drop balls into a** nonstick skillet **over medium heat. Wash hands. Cook 10 minutes, turning with a** fork **to cook through. Place on folded** paper towels **to drain, then add to** marinara sauce. **With an adult's help, cook a package of** spaghetti, **following instructions on page 50.** Spoon **sauce over noodles.**

italian garden

Chop 1 bell pepper. **Slice ½** zucchini **and ½** yellow squash **into thin rings, then cut rings in half. In a** nonstick skillet, **add 1 teaspoon** olive oil. **Toss in vegetables, and cook until soft. Pour into** marinara sauce, **and heat. With an adult's help, cook a package of** ravioletti pasta, **following instructions on page 50. Spoon sauce over noodles.**

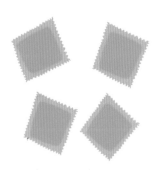

For a little extra color and flavor, top your pastas with shredded or grated Parmesan or minced parsley.

bird's-nest bowls

you will need

- 8-cup microwavable bowl
- 11-ounce package butterscotch chips
- spoon
- ½ cup creamy peanut butter
- 5-ounce can chow mein noodles
- 3 small bowls
- wax paper
- candies or treats

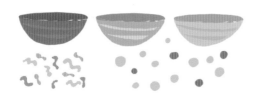

1. In a bowl, add butterscotch chips and microwave on high for 1 minute. Remove from microwave and stir. Return, heat for 15 seconds, and stir. Repeat until chips are melted.

2. Stir in peanut butter until smooth.

3. Add chow mein noodles and stir to coat with butterscotch mixture.

4. Line 3 small bowls with wax paper. Pour noodles onto wax paper, dividing noodle mixture evenly into thirds. With back of a spoon, press mixture onto sides and bottom of a bowl. Repeat for other 2 bowls.

5. Refrigerate for 1 hour. Lift by wax-paper lining out of plastic bowl.

6. Gently remove wax paper. Fill noodle bowl with M&M's or other candies. Eat bowl when candy is gone!

Tip: Try using chocolate chips or white chocolate chips, too!

Mix salty and sweet snacks in your bowls. To get even more playful, fill a nest with Marshmallow Peep chicks!

57

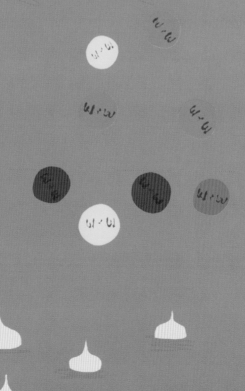
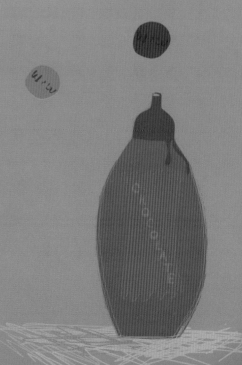

chocolate fondue

Dazzle dinner guests with this fun-due dessert!

microwave

In a small microwavable bowl, **combine** ½ **cup** semisweet chocolate chips **with 2 tablespoons** butter. **Heat for 1 minute. Stir. (Before removing bowl, check to make sure it isn't too hot to touch! If it is, let cool a few minutes.)** Microwave **for 30 seconds more. Stir well. If chocolate isn't melted, continue to heat, but stop and stir every 15 seconds. Serve warm.**

here's how!
To serve, set a bowl of fondue in the center of a table. Position treats around the "pot." Give guests a saucer and small forks, skewers, or toothpicks. Poke a treat into the dip, then eat it.

Dip with a fork
- fresh fruit
- canned pineapple
- mandarin oranges
- angel food cake slices
- dried apricots
- marshmallows
- pound cake slices

Forkless finds
- vanilla wafers
- graham crackers
- cookies
- pretzels
- potato chips
- cherries on a stem
- crackers

Almost anything tastes great covered in chocolate! Just be sure fruits are seedless—and no double-dipping!

mix-ins

For the perfect party dip, mix one of these fun flavors into the fondue recipe.

orange dream
¼ teaspoon orange extract

peanut butter kiss
¾ cup chunky peanut butter;
2 tablespoons sour cream

mint cream
3 tablespoons marshmallow crème;
¼ teaspoon peppermint extract

fruit whip
¼ cup favorite jam, jelly,
or preserves

chocolate caramel
2 tablespoons caramel
ice-cream topping

mock mounds
3 tablespoons marshmallow crème;
¼ teaspoon coconut extract

chef's journal

Kitchen Notes

Mmm! I liked these fondues best:

_____

_____

_____

_____

Next time I want to try adding

_____

_____

_____

_____

Here's my recipe:

_____

_____

_____

_____

_____

_____

_____

_____

_____

chocolate chip cookies

These cookies will have everyone saying, "Chip, chip, hurray!"

oven

1. Put rack in center of oven. Preheat oven to 350 degrees. Spray cookie sheet with cooking spray.

2. In a large bowl, combine 2 sticks (or 1 cup) softened butter, ½ cup brown sugar, ¼ cup granulated sugar, 1 egg, and ½ teaspoon vanilla. With an electric mixer, beat on a slow speed, then gradually move up to a high speed. Beat until smooth and light in color.

3. In a medium bowl, combine 2 cups all-purpose flour, ½ teaspoon baking soda, and ¼ teaspoon salt. Add flour mixture to butter mixture.

here's how!
To add flour, sprinkle ¼ cup of flour mixture over butter mixture. Using mixer, beat on low speed. Repeat ¼ cup at a time until all flour is moistened.

4. Use a spoon to stir in 1½ cups chocolate chips. As tempting as it is, don't eat raw cookie dough. It can make you sick.

5. Drop dough by heaping tablespoonfuls about 3 inches apart on cookie sheet. Bake 12 to 15 minutes or until tops of cookies begin to brown. Use oven mitt to remove cookie sheet from oven. Let cool, then use a spatula to move cookies to a wire rack.

6. Let cookie sheet cool a bit, respray, then repeat until cookie dough is gone. Makes about 2 dozen cookies.

Cookies make a great gift! Just package a mix of flavors in a colorful tin or decorated box.

mix-ins

Bake batches of gourmet cookies! Just stir in these ingredients with the chocolate chips.

double chocolate
replace ½ cup flour with
½ cup cocoa powder

berry white
1 cup white chocolate chips;
1 cup dried cranberries

double nut
¾ cup chopped pecans;
½ cup sweetened coconut flakes

peanut butter cup
¾ cup peanut butter chips;
¾ cup chopped peanuts

butterscotch bites
¾ cup butterscotch chips;
¾ cup chopped pecans

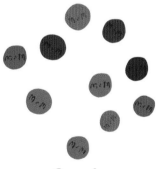

m&m chews
1 cup mini M&M's

chef's journal

Cookie Report Card
Bake these cookies, then give them a grade!

A = Awesome!

B = Better than I expected.

C = Could do in a pinch.

D = Don't even go there!

F = Fooooey!

Subject	Grade	Comments
double chocolate	☐	
berry white	☐	
double nut	☐	
peanut butter cup	☐	
butterscotch bites	☐	
m&m chews	☐	

63

chocolate pudding

Chocolate lovers will cheer for this homemade pudding.

stovetop

1. In a saucepan, combine ¾ cup sugar, 2 tablespoons cornstarch, 2 tablespoons cocoa powder, and ¼ teaspoon salt. Add 2 cups milk and stir well. With an adult's help, turn burner to medium, and place pan on it.

2. Cook for 10 minutes, stirring every minute so that milk doesn't scorch. Turn off heat, then stir in 1 tablespoon butter and 1 teaspoon vanilla. Cool slightly before pouring into dessert bowls. Chill well. Makes four ¼-cup servings.

mix-ins

Add these pudding partners to the recipe shown above for a sweet sensation!

dessert dip

Stir 4 tablespoons crunchy peanut butter into warm chocolate pudding. Pour dip into waffle bowls. Top with sprinkles. Dip in cookies, fruit, or marshmallows.

oreo mousse

Fill 4 dessert glasses with ¼ cup pudding. Crush Oreos and layer ¼ cup into each glass. Top with Cool Whip and a whole Oreo.

bear pair pudding

Sprinkle ¼ cup Gummi Bears and ¼ cup Teddy Grahams on top of each serving of chocolate pudding.

Serve Bear Pair Pudding in stemmed dessertware to show off your grrrreat taste!

chef's special!

dessert dominoes

you will need

- Fudge Shoppe Deluxe Grahams (or any rectangular chocolate-covered cookie)
- paper plate
- ½ cup white chocolate chips
- microwavable bowl
- spoon
- wooden skewer

1. Separate cookies in package. (If cookies stick together, refrigerate for a few minutes.) To remove splotches once separated, space out cookies on a paper plate, and microwave on low power for 1 minute. Let cool.

2. Microwave white chocolate chips in bowl on high for 1 minute, then stir. Heat for 15 seconds more, and stir again. Repeat until melted.

3. Dip skewer in chocolate and draw a line across each cookie. Add domino dots.

4. Press cookies onto a frosted cake or cupcakes, or serve them with a fruit salad for dessert.

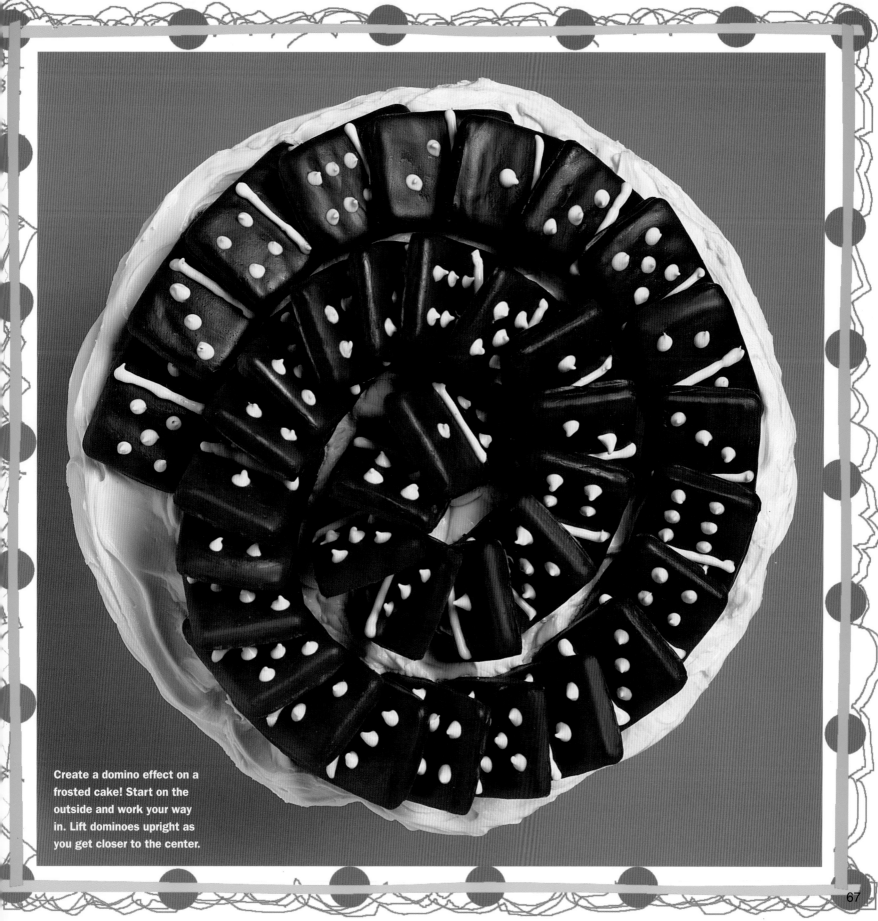

Create a domino effect on a frosted cake! Start on the outside and work your way in. Lift dominoes upright as you get closer to the center.

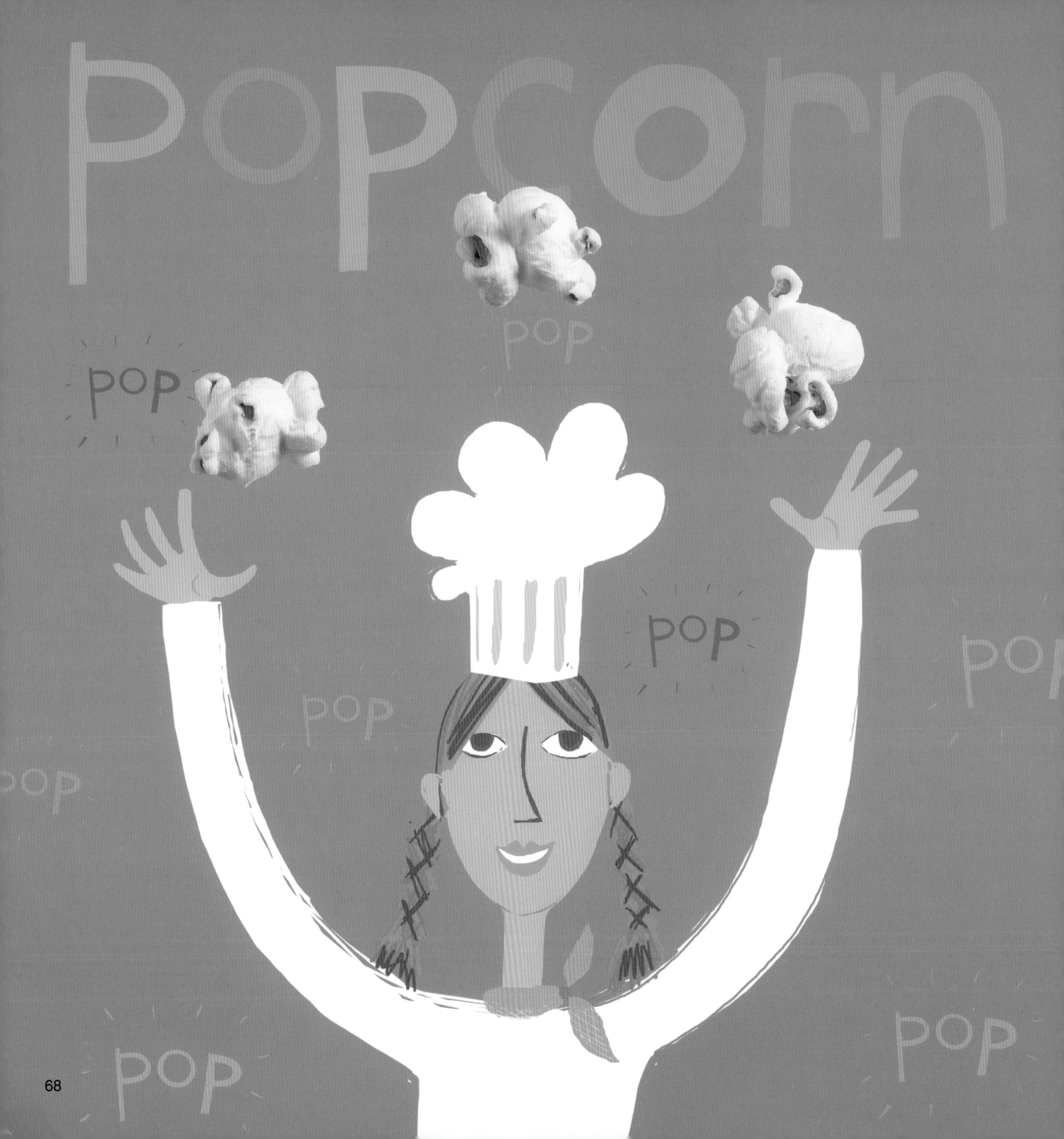
popcorn
POP
POP
POP
POP
POP
POP

old-fashioned popcorn

Let tiny kernels pop awake, then it's time to shake, shake, shake!

stovetop

1. Find a large pot with a tight-fitting lid that's not too heavy to shake.

2. Pour 3 tablespoons cooking oil and 1 or 2 kernels popcorn into pot. Set aside ½ cup of popcorn.

3. Heat on high. As soon as a kernel pops, pour the ½ cup popcorn into pan, put on lid, and slip on oven mitts.

4. With an adult's help, wait about 1 minute for popcorn to pop, then pick up pan and shake it.

here's how!

To shake popcorn, place mitted hand on lid, and lift pot with other hand. Give popcorn a hard shake a few times, return pan to the heat for 30 seconds, then pick it up and shake again. The instant popcorn stops popping, turn off the heat and remove pan. It's OK if you hear a few more kernels pop.

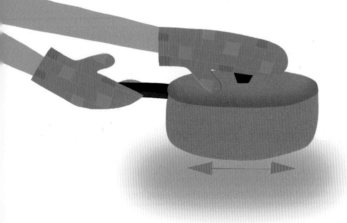

To tickle taste buds, mix a variety of popcorn flavors together.

70

mix-ins

Pour 6 cups of popped old-fashioned or microwave popcorn into a paper bag.
Add mix-ins, then seal, shake, and serve.

cheese pleaser
**2 tablespoons powdered
cheese topping**

kettle korn
**¼ cup sugar;
½ teaspoon cinnamon**

tex mix
**1 teaspoon taco
seasoning; 2 tablespoons
powdered cheese topping**

movie madness
1 cup Milk Duds

pucker popper
1 teaspoon dry ranch dressing mix

peanut butter cup
**½ cup chocolate chips;
½ cup peanut butter chips**

Popcorn Stand
Take notes of your friends' and family's
favorite flavored popcorn. On a birthday
or other special day, pop up a big bag
and serve it in a colorful tin.

guest check

Name	Favorite Popcorn	Comments

popcorn balls

Have a ball making these marshmallowy treats!

stovetop

1. Melt 3 tablespoons butter **in a** large nonstick saucepan **over medium-low heat. Add a 10-ounce package of miniature or 40 regular-sized** marshmallows, **and stir constantly to melt. Remove from heat.**

2. Add 6 cups popped popcorn. **Stir with** wooden spoon **to coat popcorn with marshmallows. When cool enough to touch, butter your hands and shape popcorn into tennis-ball-sized balls. Lay on** wax paper. **Makes about 10 balls.**

mix-ins

Stir these sweet—and surprising—extras into the marshmallow mixture along with the popcorn.

fuddy nutty

Coat a medium saucepan **with** cooking spray. **Turn burner to medium-high heat, then toss in** ½ cup raw slivered almonds **and** ½ cup coconut flakes. **Continue to stir with a** wooden spoon **until coconut has a tan color. Let cool. Pour coconut and almonds into** marshmallow recipe **along with popcorn. Stir, then shape into balls.**

confetti balls

Chop 1 cup gumdrops **into small pieces with a** butter knife. **Mix candy and 1 cup** fruit-flavored cereal **into** marshmallow recipe **along with popcorn. Stir, then shape into balls.**

crunch bars

Pour ½ cup raisins, **1 cup** peanuts, **and ½ teaspoon** cinnamon **into** marshmallow recipe **along with popcorn. Butter a** loaf pan, **and press mixture into it. Cut into bars with a** butter knife.

For decoration, form a popcorn ball around a licorice string and decorate with a bow.

chef's special!

garden pops

you will need

- popcorn ball recipe from page 72
- butter or cooking spray
- wax paper
- popsicle sticks
- ready-made frosting
- red gumdrops
- small green jelly beans
- red food coloring
- red licorice strings
- red sugar
- small brown jelly beans
- kitchen scissors
- yellow fruit roll-ups

1. Read instructions for flower you're making before starting, because you may want to add food coloring to popcorn mixture.

2. Make popcorn ball recipe, but don't shape into balls.

3. Working quickly before mixture gets hard, butter hands or coat them with cooking spray. Shape flowers on wax paper while mixture is sticky. Insert popsicle sticks into flowers, then let lie flat until popcorn hardens.

daisy

Shape a large center ball. Stick smaller balls around large ball. Press flower flat. Add frosting to center, then press on gumdrops. Place green jelly beans around center next to gumdrops.

tulip

Turn marshmallow mixture pink by adding red food coloring to mixture before adding popcorn. Roll popcorn mixture into 3 ropes 4 inches long and 1 inch wide. Pinch one end of each rope to form a point. For tulip base, bring other ends together, and press them flat two-thirds of way up rope. Use frosting to hold licorice around edges. Sprinkle with red sugar.

sunflower

Shape a 3-inch ball, then flatten it. For "seeds," fill center with frosting, then cover it with brown jelly beans. Cut petal shapes with scissors from fruit roll-ups and place petals around edge of flower center.

For a party, cut a sheet of green
paper or wax paper for the table.
Arrange flowers on top.

ice cream

76

ice cream

girlie-swirlie shakes

Create a thick vanilla shake from ice cream you can make!

blender

Pour ½ cup milk into a blender. Add 1 or 2 scoops freezer ice cream (see recipe below) or store-bought vanilla ice cream. Cover, blend on high until smooth, then pour into a glass. Top with whipped cream, if desired. Serves 1 to 2.

freezer ice cream

1. Combine 1 cup cold milk, 1 cup heavy whipping cream, ⅔ cup sugar, and 1 teaspoon vanilla in a shallow container that will fit into freezer.

2. Stir awhile, until sugar dissolves. Cover with lid or plastic wrap, and place in freezer.

3. After 2 hours, stir ice cream to break up any crystals. Ice cream will be soft and can be eaten at this point or returned to freezer to get firmer. Let soften 5 minutes before serving. Serves 4.

Serve your shakes, like this Pink Flamingo, in cool glasses with colorful straws!

78

mix-ins

To make a super shake, add these ingredients to 1 or 2 scoops ice cream!

chocolate monkey

replace vanilla ice cream with chocolate; ½ cup milk; 1 large peanut butter cup; ½ banana

maple milk shake

**½ cup milk;
1 tablespoon maple syrup;
2 tablespoons toffee bits**

soy power plus

**replace ice cream with chocolate soy ice cream, such as Tofutti;
½ cup chocolate soy milk;
1 frozen banana;
2 tablespoons peanut butter**

cookies 'n' cream

½ cup cold milk; 2 tablespoons chocolate syrup; 2 Oreos

white whopper

**½ cup milk; ½ cup Whoppers malted milk balls;
2 tablespoons chocolate syrup**

pink flamingo

½ cup cold milk; ½ cup fresh or frozen strawberries, sliced

chef's journal

Four-Star Reviews

After blending up these super shakes, rate them! Write the number of stars you think they rate in the boxes. Ask friends and family to vote for their favorites!

★ ★ ★ ★ A superstar!

★ ★ ★ This dish shines!

★ ★ Needs more polish.

★ Too dull to delight.

chocolate monkey

maple milk shake

soy power plus

cookies 'n' cream

white whopper

pink flamingo

ice cream sandwiches

Dip away for this dreamy ice cream treat!

freezer

1. Soften a pint of chocolate chip cookie dough ice cream for 5 minutes.

2. Place a scoop of ice cream between 2 soft chocolate chip cookies. Repeat until you've used all the ice cream.

3. Roll edges of each sandwich in mini chocolate chips.

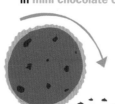

4. After you've made sandwiches, cover them with plastic wrap, then refreeze until they're firm.

Invent your own ice cream sandwich! Try different ice cream and cookie flavors.

mix-ins

Fix a fantastic frozen treat by combining a few of your favorite flavors!

mint cooler
peppermint pattie candies, frozen;
mint chocolate chip ice cream

oatburst
2 soft oatmeal cookies; vanilla ice
cream or soy vanilla ice cream

mini rainbow
colored vanilla wafers;
French vanilla ice cream;
roll edges in candy sprinkles

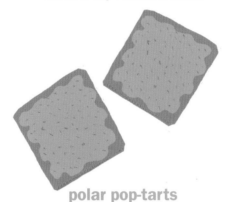

polar pop-tarts
Pop-Tarts cut in half;
fruit-flavored ice cream

gooey grahams
chocolate-covered
graham cracker cookies;
strawberry ice cream;
banana slices

brrrr-berry
thin chocolate wafer cookies;
raspberry ice cream;
small scoop of Cool Whip

chef's journal

Kitchen Notes

Mmm! I liked these ice cream
sandwiches best:

Next time I want to try adding

Here's my recipe:

chef's special!

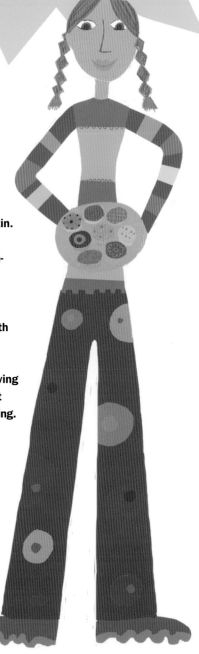

very cool cupcakes

you will need

- **2 pints ice cream (any flavor)**
- **paper cupcake liners**
- **muffin tin**
- **spoon**
- **food coloring**
- **vanilla frosting**
- **sprinkles**
- **sugars**
- **candies**

1. Let ice cream soften for about 30 minutes.

2. Place cupcake liners in a muffin tin.

3. Spoon softened ice cream into liners. Freeze until solid.

4. For fun colors, add food coloring to vanilla frosting, then decorate with sprinkles, sugars, and candies.

Tip: Plan topping ideas before removing cupcakes from freezer, so they don't melt too quickly while you're decorating.

mix
a
meal

drinks

These special sippers will suit any meal. Serve thick drinks with light meals and light drinks with heavier dishes.

eye-opener smoothie

Mix **1 cup** orange juice, **1** banana, **and 1 tablespoon** honey
in a blender **on medium speed. With blender running, remove
plastic spout (but keep on lid!) and add 1 cup** frozen strawberries,
a few at a time, blending until smooth. Serves 1 to 2.

sparkling lemonade

Pour lemon-lime soda **into a** glass. **Squeeze juice from**
½ lemon **into drink. (Strain out seeds!) Add ice cubes. Serves 1.**

fruit frappé

Cut tops off 7 fresh strawberries. **Slice berries and put in**
freezer **for 1 hour. In a** blender, **add strawberries, 1 small container
of** lemon custard-style yogurt, **and ⅓ cup** orange juice.
Blend until smooth. Serves 1.

pineapple punch

Pour ½ cup pineapple juice **and ½ cup** orange juice **into**
small pitcher. **Add 1 scoop softened** orange sherbet. **Stir to blend.
Top with 1 cup** ginger ale. **Serves 2.**

mango lhassi

Mix 1 cup each of plain yogurt **and** mango sorbet **in a**
blender **until smooth. (You may use any flavor of sorbet.)
Serves 1 to 2.**

cranberry splash

Pour ½ cup each of chilled cranberry juice, pineapple juice,
and ginger ale **into a** tall glass. **Serves 1.**

Choose a glass, garnish, straw, or swizzle stick that fits the style of your drink, such as the Pineapple Punch, Cranberry Splash, Sparkling Lemonade, and Mango Lhassi.

soups and salads

These dishes make soup-er starters! Choose one that complements your main dish.

italian flag salad

In a large bowl, **mix 1 cup sliced** roma tomatoes, **1 cup cubed** mozzarella cheese, **¼ cup chopped** fresh basil leaves, **and ¼ cup** Italian dressing. **Chill. Serves 2 to 4.**

bits-and-bites salad

Wash and dry 10-ounce bag of European salad greens **or 4 cups of** iceberg lettuce. **Place in a** large bowl. **Sprinkle ¾ cup** dried cranberries, **½ cup finely chopped** jicama, **½ cup finely chopped** carrots, **and ¼ cup** sliced almonds. **Toss with ¼ cup** Paul Newman's Balsamic Vinaigrette **(or your favorite salad dressing). Serves 4.**

bunny slaw

In a large bowl, **mix 6 grated** carrots, **1 cup drained** crushed pineapple, **1 cup** golden raisins, **and 1 cup** mayonnaise. **Chill. Serves 6.**

cream of broccoli

Heat a 10-ounce box of frozen broccoli florets, **following directions on package. Drain well. In** medium pot, **combine 1 can** cream of chicken soup, **½ cup grated** Parmesan cheese, **and 2 cups** milk **over medium heat. Add broccoli. Heat until small bubbles break on surface. Serves 4.**

quick tomato topper

In a medium pot, **heat 1 can of** tomato soup, **following directions on can. Pour into a** bowl. **Add a dollop of** sour cream **on top. Garnish with chopped** green onions. **Serves 2.**

hot potato! soup

With an adult's help, pour a 14-ounce can of vegetable broth **into a** medium saucepan. **Heat on medium-high. After the soup starts to boil, stir in ½ cup** instant mashed potato flakes, **such as Potato Buds, and a dash of** salt and pepper. **Remove from heat. Use more flakes if you want a thicker soup. Chop up 1 can of** new potatoes **for more potato flavor!**

Fill a pastry or plastic bag with sour cream. Squeeze simple doodles into a bowl of tomato soup for someone special.

simple sides

Although these sides taste like you spent lots of time in the kitchen, they're simple to make!

fruit kabobs

Slide a watermelon **chunk, a** green grape, **a** peach **slice,
a** strawberry, **and a** kiwi **chunk onto a 6-inch** wooden skewer.
Place raspberry yogurt **into a** small bowl. **Chill. To eat,
dip fruit in yogurt. Serves 1.**

hash browns

In a large skillet, **heat 2 tablespoons** cooking oil **over
medium-high heat. Add 3 cups frozen, shredded** hash brown
potatoes, **½ cup chopped** onion, **and ½ teaspoon** salt, **then lower
heat to medium. Cook for 5 to 7 minutes, stirring and flipping with
a** spatula, **until potatoes are browned and tender. Serves 2.**

pink clouds

In a large bowl, **mix a 3-ounce box** raspberry gelatin **powder
(not sugar-free) and a 23-ounce jar** natural applesauce. **Chill.
Stir in an 8-ounce container thawed** Cool Whip
before serving. Serves 6.

celery stuffers

In a small bowl, **mix ¼ cup shredded** cheddar cheese,
1 tablespoon cream cheese, **and 1 tablespoon** salsa. **Spread
cheese mixture onto a** celery stalk. **Serve** peanut butter **and**
fruit-flavored cream cheese **on separate stalks. Serves 1 to 3.**

six-star salad

In a large bowl, **mix 1 can** mandarin oranges, **drained, 1 cup**
sweetened coconut flakes, **1 cup** crushed drained pineapple,
1 cup miniature marshmallows, **1 cup** sour cream, **and 1 cup**
chopped pecans. **Chill. Serves 6.**

fried corn

Heat 2 cups frozen corn **in** microwave, **following package
instructions. Melt 2 tablespoons** butter **in a** nonstick skillet
over medium heat. Add corn and 1 small diced onion. **Stir
corn until butter disappears and onions are crispy.
Season with** salt and pepper. **Serves 2 to 4.**

If you're in the mood for a sweet-and-sour side dish, the Six-Star Salad shines!

91

sweets

Do something sweet for the ones you love—starting or ending with these yummy sides!

mud puddles

Stir 3 tablespoons peanut butter **with ¼ cup** pancake syrup. **Break off pieces of** biscuit **or** bread slices **and dip them into mud puddle. Serves 1.**

candied marshmallows

Stick a toothpick **into a** large marshmallow. **Dip top of marshmallow into** milk, **then into** Jell-O **powder. Place a mix of flavors on a** tray, **and serve as appetizers.**

sunrise salute

In a tall glass, **layer ½ cup each of** vanilla yogurt, blueberries, **and** raspberries, **and ¼ cup** Rice Krispies. **Top with more yogurt and a few blueberries. Serves 1.**

peanutty crisp

Cut an apple **in half. Cut out the core. Spread 1 tablespoon** peanut butter **on each half. Sprinkle on 1 teaspoon each of** raisins **and** granola. **Serves 2.**

jell-o jewels

Make Jell-O, **following instructions on a 6-ounce box. Pour liquid Jell-O into** mini gelatin molds. **Let set in refrigerator for 15 to 20 minutes, then press drained,** canned fruit **or** fresh fruit **into Jell-O. Chill until firm. To remove Jell-O from mold, dip pan into hot tap water, then turn mold over onto** serving dish. **Serves 6.**

iced cranberry creams

Place tinfoil cupcake liners **into a** muffin tin. **Mix 1 can** jellied cranberry sauce **with 2 tablespoons** lemon juice. **Divide among 12 cups. Blend together 4-ounce package** cream cheese, **4 tablespoons** mayonnaise, **and 4 tablespoons** powdered sugar. **Add ½ cup** Cool Whip. **Spoon onto** cranberry sauce. **Place in freezer. Serve frozen.**

Add a little wiggle to your meal with mix-and-match Jell-O flavors and fruits! Use mini molds for individual Jell-O jewels.

set a basic table

Dine in style with a table setting that's perfect for the meal you're serving!

Plan to serve bread? Add a
small plate and butter knife.

Turn the knife blade
toward the plate.

If you're planning a salad, add
a salad fork—otherwise, just
a dinner fork is fine.

Place a spoon on the table if
you're serving soup, a liquidy
food, or dessert. Otherwise,
you can skip it!

show-off tabletops

Simple touches on the table will make a special day shine!

birthday

Sprinkle confetti all around a bright tablecloth. Set the table with a mix of colorful plates and cups. Write sweet sayings on metal-rim key tags, tie tags to colorful candy bracelets, then slip bracelets around napkins. Freeze colorful juices in ice cube trays for drinks.

valentine's day

Fill white teacups with red candies, licorice whips, and lollipops, then tie red ribbons around teacup handles. Place a mix of pink, red, and purple napkins on the table. Lay paper doilies on bread plates, slip a heart-shaped cookie on top, and serve one to each guest.

mother's day

On a serving tray, fill a small basket with a variety of Mom's favorite teas. Place jam in a pretty dish. Fill a teacup with rose blooms (no stems!). Tie a pink linen napkin with a lime ribbon, and bundle tea cookies with a lacy ribbon. Wrap potpourri in a lacy handkerchief.

father's day

Lay a blue-and-white-plaid napkin or place mat onto a serving tray. Remove the label from a tin can and fill it with purple and blue wildflowers. Add pebbles to hold the flowers in place. Slip your picture into a silver frame and place it on the serving tray.

fourth of july

Cover the table with blue construction paper, then scatter red and white crayons for guests to use to write messages on the paper. Bundle plasticware inside a white napkin and tie up with red, white, and blue curling ribbon. Make a patriotic centerpiece with balloons.

halloween

Slip bottles of orange soda into a black plastic beach pail, and fill pail with ice. Decorate terra-cotta pots, then fill with spooky treats. Stretch cotton or fake cobwebs under tableware or over chair backs. Write guests' names on tiny pumpkins with a black marker. Hide plastic spiders around the table.

Attention all chefs!
Once you've mastered the Mix-Ins, send us your own culinary creations.

Send recipes to:
***The Mix-It-Up Cookbook* Editor**
American Girl Library
8400 Fairway Place
Middleton, WI 53562

Special thanks to all of our chefs:

Anna G., Oklahoma • Briana M., California

Caroline D., California • Caroline P., Michigan

Christina M., Virginia • Christine Y., New Jersey

Claire D., California • Devyn S., California

Dorothy M., Oregon • Elizabeth P., Washington

Emily D., Pennsylvania • Emma W., Indiana

Hannah G., California • Jenny N., Maryland

Jessie L., Texas • Julia R., New Jersey

Kaitlyn B., Illinois • Katie D., Virginia

Lindsay S., Massachusetts • Marion H., California

Mollee H., Washington • Molly K., Massachusetts

Natasha D., California • Nicole R., Wisconsin

Perri M., Connecticut • Rebekah N., Maryland

Sam D., Wisconsin • Shelby S., Louisiana

Taylor B., Wisconsin • Tylynn V., Wisconsin • Zoe B., California

Try it risk-free!

American Girl® magazine is especially for girls 8 and up. Send for your preview issue today! Mail this card to receive a risk-free preview issue and start your one-year subscription. For just $19.95, you'll receive 6 bimonthly issues in all! If you don't love it right away, just write "cancel" on the invoice and return it to us. The preview issue is yours to keep, free!

Send bill to: (please print)

Adult's name

Address

City   State   Zip

Adult's signature

Send magazine to: (please print)

Girl's name   Birthdate *(optional)*

Address

City   State   Zip